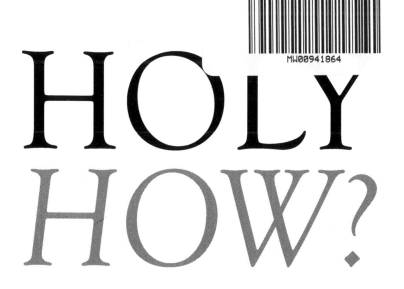

HOLY HOW?

HOLINESS, THE SABBATH, COMMUNION AND BAPTISM

*Celebrating God's Provision While Escaping
Lingering Shadows of Dark Ages Thinking*

Ben R. Peters

HOLY — HOW?
HOLINESS, THE SABBATH, COMMUNION AND BAPTISM
© 2013 by Ben R. Peters

Published by
Kingdom Sending Center
P. O. Box 25
Genoa, IL 60135

www.kingdomsendingcenter.org
ben.peters@kingdomsendingcenter.org

ISBN 13: 978-1494436421

Cover image: courtesy of *www.BartowImages.com*
Cover and book design by *www.ChristianBookDesign.com*

Contents

PREFACE 5

Chapter 1   ESCAPING THE SHADOWS OF THE SHROUD 7

Chapter 2   HOLY, HOLY, HOLY 15

Chapter 3   THE BOUNTIFUL BLESSINGS OF HOLINESS 21

Chapter 4   THE JOY OF HOLINESS IN TIMES
             OF RESTORATION 33

Chapter 5   THE PRECIOUS GIFTS OF THE SABBATH
             AND THE FIRST DAY 43

Chapter 6   COMMUNION — WHAT WE'VE BEEN MISSING 61

Chapter 7   THE BLESSINGS OF BAPTISM 79

Chapter 8   APPLICATION OF REVELATION 89

Preface

What can be said about Holiness, the Sabbath, Communion and Baptism that hasn't been said before in sermons, books and theological debates? Who do I think I am to have anything to add to these subjects when so many esteemed theologians and biblical scholars have devoted their brilliant minds to examine these important doctrines?

While I do have a good background in the Scriptures, the ideas put forward in this book are not based entirely on Biblical scholarship, *per se*. Rather they emanate from a combination of a life in the Word, an awareness that God hasn't finished with the Reformation or Restoration of His church, and specific times of special insights when God chooses to download tidbits of truth that suddenly makes sense of things that never made sense before.

So to be very clear, I don't claim to be the final authority or even the most scholarly expert on these subjects. I do, however, claim to be privileged, as a child of the King of Kings, to have special access to inside information, hanging out with the Father, Jesus and the Holy Spirit, in the courts of the Most High God. It's in those special times of hanging out together, that insights, revelation and wisdom flow into my spirit, and I get very excited about God's amazing ways. I'm sure you've experienced those special times as well. We all have the same opportunity to come boldly into His Throne Room.

This book is designed to help the church of Jesus Christ to blow away more of the Medieval dust that still clouds our minds with Dark Ages thinking. It's designed to get you updated and upgraded by the Holy Spirit of God, Who inspired both the Reformation and the Restoration of all things that were lost in those Dark Ages. They were not called the Dark Ages by chance. The light of the good news (the gospel) had almost gone out in Medieval times. Today, the light is growing stronger and stronger and more and more darkness is being overpowered by the light of the Spirit of Restoration.

I trust the revelation of God's love unveiled in the doctrines discussed in this book will thrill you as much as they have thrilled me. It is my privilege to share my joy with you as Jesus delights in sharing His joy with all of us.

May God open your heart and mind and transform your life, as you meditate on the following revolutionary ideas with me.

Chapter One

Escaping the Shadows
of the Shroud

"You are not holy. You need to be quiet. This is a holy place." The lady speaking happened to be a Catholic nun from an Asian country. The "holy place" happened to be the Upper Room in Jerusalem, where it is believed that Jesus shared His Last Supper with the twelve disciples, and where The Holy Spirit was poured out on the one hundred and twenty followers of the risen Lord.

It was just a few years ago. I was blessed to be a part of a very wonderful experience in the land of Israel. There were exactly thirty-seven of us, just as God had spoken to one of our leaders, Lisa Bourland, of Henderson, Kentucky. Supresa Sithole, a Mozambiquan leader of Iris Ministries, under Heidi and Rolland Baker, had prophesied that thirty-seven prayer warriors would meet in the prayer room that Lisa had visited and prophesy to the dry bones of the House of Israel, as recorded in Ezekiel 37.

You see, on an incredible journey of obedience to the voice

of the Holy Spirit, Lisa had gone to Israel and walked through every open door that God gave her. Through miraculous and divine encounters, she was taken to an old and long-neglected prayer room in the basement of the YMCA Hotel in Jerusalem.

Given permission to linger and pray there, she heard The Lord say, "Lisa, count the chairs in this room."

Lisa obeyed. There were thirty-seven chairs.

Again, she heard God say, "Lisa, count the chairs again."

Thinking she may have counted wrong, she counted again. There were still thirty-seven chairs.

Not attaching any significance to that number, she communicated with Supresa, who had given her the original word to go to Israel for a gift that God had waiting for her there.

Hearing the above account, Supresa replied with his unique accent: "Sista, it's Ezekiel thahty-seven. You will bring thahty-seven prophetic prayer warriors, who will prophesy to the dry bones of the house of Israel in that room."

It happened without any human manipulation. Lisa Bourland shared the story in several groups of people. Some committed to come, but later backed out. Others decided to come at the last minute. The last to arrive was a flight attendant who was flying on standby. There were no seats available that week, but suddenly a seat opened up to her and when we counted heads in Jerusalem, at the end of the day on the day we arrived, the count came to exactly thirty-seven.

We prayed and prophesied throughout the nights in two-hour shifts, both in the prayer room and in the watch tower overlooking much of the city. During the daytime, we toured the famous sites in the city, until we came to the place, which is believed to be the very site of the biblical upper room.

This was where we got in trouble with the precious little nun and her companions. You see, we were feeling the presence of the same Holy Spirit that visited the one hundred, twenty disciples about two thousand years ago. We weren't being really wild or crazy. We were just worshipping out loud, some in an unknown language, while a few of us were laying on the floor or walking around with our hands in the air and God's praises in our mouths.

It was obvious that the nun's definition of holiness was sober silence. Of course, we didn't argue theology, or discuss what happened in that place on the Day of Pentecost. Instead, we graciously moved on so they could occupy the space and be properly "holy".

The experience left us feeling sorry for the millions of people still living in the shadows of the Dark Ages. How we desire that God will reveal Himself to them and set them free from the bondage of relationless religion.

SHADOWS OF THE SHROUD

The shadows of the shroud of the Dark Ages still linger over the church in the twenty-first century. They still cloud our vision and permeate our religious concepts. There are very few religious notions more affected by this than the notion that holiness is a heavy and somber assignment, given to those who would try to please a powerful and vengeful God. Those who pursue a life of holiness, must surely become like mystics or monks or both, becoming totally separated from any kind of worldly activities.

For some groups, this means not using modern transportation. For some it means not wearing a tie. For some it means women must wear ankle length dresses and never cut their hair. For still others, holiness is not smoking, drinking, chewing, dancing or going to movie theaters.

A relative by marriage had a family member kicked out of the group because he used a chain saw, instead of a hand saw. He even used an electric one because it was quieter and he hoped that no one would hear it and report him. There are a lot more examples, but the point has been made. The details may change from group to group, but for the most part the underlying thought is that pleasure is evil and separating yourself from society and being sad and somber is holy.

As we shall quickly see in a multitude of Scriptures, there is nothing further from the truth. Holiness was never a heavy burden to bear—rather it was an exciting privilege meant to be valued and joyfully embraced. Any other approach or attitude is the result of the shadow of the shroud that still lingers over the church.

The attitude and confusion in the church towards the Sabbath is also the result of our religious heritage, not only from the Dark Ages, but also from the religious Jewish history dating back to Old Testament times. Scribes and Pharisees made the Sabbath a heavy burden to bear.

We will demonstrate the fact that Jesus meant what He said when He declared that God made the Sabbath for man rather than man for the Sabbath. When we see the purpose and plan of God in giving us the Sabbath, we will more joyfully praise and worship Him for His incredible wisdom and lavish love for us.

It's not our purpose here to do a detailed history lesson on the Dark Ages. There are many great resources for that. We simply want to provide some obvious conclusions from general knowledge to make our point.

The main point we want to make is that in the dark ages, people knew little about a personal relationship with God. Christianity, very much like Judaism, had degenerated into a religious organization, where followers were told by human leaders what they must do to qualify for the benefits of their religion.

Leaders of the religion enjoyed the power of controlling what the people did, using both the carrot and the stick approaches to ensure compliance. This manifested in doctrines and practices such as Purgatory (a temporary place of punishment), and the Indulgences, which have various meanings throughout church history. Basically, however, the Indulgences were the means by which the penalty and guilt for sin could be removed from the sinner if they would pay a certain amount of money to the priest or bishop, etc. Often, it was used to get the sinner out of Purgatory sooner. This abuse of power enabled church leaders to gain wealth and even more control over the lives of the common people.

Fear is a tool of every religious cult leader, and the church of the Dark Ages was in so many ways like religious cults that we see today. People were afraid to say anything negative about the church and it's practices. It took some brave leaders to bring about the Reformation, many of whom would lay down their lives to begin the process of the great Restoration of the true church of Jesus Christ.

The fear that was put on people in the Dark Ages was in harmony with the attitude people still have regarding holiness. People were told that to be holy, they had to be sober and serious and give up almost every pleasure known to man. They were threatened with more time in purgatory and even excommunication from the church if they failed to conform. This of course would mean certain eternal punishment in hell.

It's no wonder that holiness has a negative and burdensome attachment to the very mention of the word. During the Reformation process, God raised up Reformers like John Wesley, who did much to reform the concept of holiness. Sadly, however, the movement he founded slipped back into the older, more accepted way of thinking regarding this important subject. In the chapters to follow, we will share more about how this amazing man of God taught people some great insights about true holiness.

Regarding the doctrine of Communion, I am seriously surprised that the church has not yet escaped the shadows of the shroud covering this wonderful doctrine. I am referring to the sober and even morbid focus on the pain and suffering experienced by Jesus on the cross and His journey to Calvary.

The powerful movie, *The Passion*, directed by Mel Gibson, clearly illustrates this fact. While this movie was a great tool to reveal how much God loves us, it still conveys a Dark Ages focus and leaves us with heavy hearts, even though it finishes briefly with the fact of the Resurrection. Obviously, the creator of the movie felt that this was what was appropriate. Jesus certainly suffered incredibly on our behalf, and that point was very powerfully made.

My point is not that *The Passion* should not have shown us how much Jesus suffered. What it lacked, however, was any significant focus on what Jesus accomplished for us. When we look at the purpose and meaning of Communion, we will see that Jesus was not telling His disciples to feel His pain as much as He was revealing to them that His pain was their great gain.

The spirit of the Dark Ages was a heavy and somber shroud over a people kept in darkness. They had no Bibles in their own languages. Mass was done in Latin and most did not understand it at all. The people were at the mercy of their leaders and many of their leaders wanted to keep it that way. The doctrine of the suffering and death of Jesus was a chief focus of the church in those days. They wore the crucifix with Jesus still on the cross. It was a religion associated with pain and sorrow, and holiness was attached to being sad and suffering with Jesus.

Still today, many Communion services are somber ceremonies with little or no joy attached. We are warned about taking Communion without first confessing any lingering sin, lest we be suddenly taken out in a moment of God's fierce wrath. I trust we can bring some understanding to this great and wonderful practice in the pages ahead.

The practice of baptism, while usually a much happier ceremony, is still a subject for great controversy and confusion, rather than a symbol of great opportunity to fulfill a great destiny. We will share some insights on this practice that should get you very excited.

So please come with me on an exciting journey into some unexpected good news. These four important church doctrines are truly loaded with hidden treasures of great value, bringing great joy and power to the Bride of Christ, His Body, His Church.

Chapter Two

Holy, Holy, Holy

A KIND OF SCARY COMMANDMENT

We've all probably felt a little overwhelmed when we've read, or heard preached, the verse that says, "Be ye holy, for I am holy!" (KJV). Peter quotes this word from God recorded in Leviticus 11:44,45 in I Peter 1:16. The context does indeed talk about moral purity and leaving behind the culture of the heathen, but I do believe Peter also had a balanced view of holiness, as reflected in some of his other comments. His exhortation to be holy, like God was holy, had to include more than not doing sinful things.

Peter was well aware that God's holiness had very little to do with Him not doing bad things. Peter clearly demonstrated the more complete and balanced understanding of holiness, as he walked in the love and power of a holy God, empowered by the Holy Spirit, preaching a holy gospel about the holy Son of

God. As we look at the actual meaning of the word, we will be encouraged that being holy is an awesome privilege and a glorious opportunity to participate in the powerful work and the beautiful character of the Creator of the universe.

DEFINING THE TERM

Let's begin by taking a broad and balanced look at some definitions of the word, "holy". Let's look first at the Miriam Webster's English usage definition:

ho·ly\ ʹhō-lē\
adjective
1. exalted or worthy of complete devotion as one perfect in goodness and righteousness
2. divine <for the Lord our God is *holy* — Psalms 99:9 (Authorized Version)>
3. devoted entirely to the deity or the work of the deity <a *holy* temple> <*holy* prophets>
4a. having a divine quality <*holy* love>
   b. venerated as or as if sacred <*holy* scripture> <a *holy* relic>
5. —used as an intensive <this is a *holy* mess> <he was a *holy* terror when he drank — Thomas Wolfe>; often used in combination as a mild oath <*holy* smoke>
Other forms: ho·li·er; ho·li·est

ho·li·ly \-lə-lē\ adverb
Examples
the *holy* monk spent many hours on his knees in prayer
the Torah contains the *holy* writings of Judaism

the *Holy* Trinity

Origin: Middle English, from Old English *hālig*; akin to Old English *hāl* whole — more at whole.

First use: before 12th century

Synonyms: devout, godly, pious, religious, sainted, saintly

Antonyms: antireligious, faithless, godless, impious, irreligious, ungodly, unholy

As you can clearly see, the word, "holy", is used in a number of different ways, describing people, places and things, as well as God, Himself. For our understanding of how we as God's children are to be holy, I think the third and fourth definitions have the clearest meanings and applications.

"Devoted entirely to deity or the work of the deity" actually reveals the most essential element of the word, "holy." It has to do with being devoted to or set apart for. We will see this clearly as we now look at the Hebrew and Greek definitions.

Here is the meaning of "holy" from a dictionary of Hebrew words.

קדש

qôdesh

Definition:

1) apartness, holiness, sacredness, separateness

1a) apartness, sacredness, holiness

1a1) of God

1a2) of places

1a3) of things

1b) set-apartness, separateness

Part of Speech: noun masculine

A Related Word by BDB/Strong's Number: from H6942
Same Word by TWOT Number: 1990a

Here we have a simple and to-the-point definition of holiness. Holy means to be set apart, or as I like to put it: "In a class by itself." It means special and dedicated or consecrated for a special purpose.

Now let's look at the Greek definition:

hagion
Thayer Definition:
1) reverend, worthy of veneration
1a) of things which on account of some connection with God possess a certain distinction and claim to reverence, as places sacred to God which are not to be profaned
1b) of persons whose services God employs, for example, apostles
2) set apart for God, to be as it were, exclusively his
3) services and offerings
3a) prepared for God with solemn rite, pure, clean
4) in a moral sense, pure sinless upright holy
Part of Speech: adjective
A Related Word by Thayer's/Strong's Number: neuter of 1G40

As we can see, there is not a lot of differences between the English, Hebrew and Greek definitions.

There is clearly an element of purity and separation from evil things in the meaning of "holy", but there is also without doubt the element of being special, even exalted or favored in the meaning. The most basic element of the definition is the "set-apartness" aspect.

To be set apart usually means something very positive, although it could also mean set apart for punishment. The sad thing about the way this word's meaning has evolved and come to us is that the church in the Dark Ages focused almost completely on the negative aspects of holiness forgetting or ignoring the more positive aspects.

Let's Use a Little Logic for a Minute

If we are to be holy as God is holy, we need to understand what it means for God to be holy.

How is God Holy?

I asked for help from a small congregation when I recently spoke on this subject. I asked them what it meant for God to be set apart or different from other gods. Surely, it was not the fact that He didn't smoke or drink or do drugs, etc. What makes our God different than other gods?

The first answer encapsulated the truth of God's holiness or "set-apartness". A lady said that it was His power and His love. I gave her a perfect A+ for her answer. What makes God special is that He is all-powerful and He is love.

So then, if we are to be holy, like God is holy, then shouldn't we also be different from others in our world by being powerful and full of love. It is true that as God's children we get to live free from the bondage of sin, which is a good thing (certainly not a heavy burden), but it is just as true that we should possess power to do supernatural things for others, like Jesus did, and we should be full of God's love, just like Jesus was.

After all, was not Jesus the human expression of the Father in Heaven? He did say that if we've seen Him, we've seen the Father. To be holy then, as God is holy, is to be just like Jesus, who was our "on-earth" example of what God was like. Then Jesus called us His Body—the new on-earth example of what God is like.

A religious people without a real relationship with Jesus will always look for rules and ceremonies to follow, so they can be holy and accepted by an impersonal and judgmental god. But people who are truly holy as God is holy look for intimacy with Him as He does with us, and they seek a transfer of His power and love into their lives so they can actually do what He does as an extension of Him on the earth.

The sad and tragic truth is that there is a very natural tendency and carnal motivation for both leaders and followers to slip and slide into an inferior meaning and understanding of a term like holiness.

Leaders, who have inferior motives, are usually in favor of a more legalistic meaning because it gives them more control over the people. Followers, who just want to be safe from judgment, like a legalistic meaning because it means that they can do something religious without having to pursue a deeper relationship with God.

In order for us to overcome our natural flesh and spiritual laziness, we need to take a good look at what we have to gain by pursuing true holiness. You may be very surprised and amazed by what you read in the following pages.

Chapter Three

The Bountiful Blessings of Holiness

B iblical scholars love to use the principle of "first mention" in the Bible to attach special meaning to a particular verse. In other words, they find the first time a certain word or subject was mentioned in Scripture, and they pay special attention to how it was used.

Of the 611 times the word "holy" is used in the Bible, the first reference is found in Exodus 3:5. In this well known story, God speaks to Moses out of the burning bush and tells him to take off his shoes, because the place where he was standing was holy ground.

Based on this famous passage, I found several wonderful blessings that God brought with Him, when he gave Moses this unique encounter in a very unusual "holy place."

1. Holiness Involves the Unexpected, Not the Mundane

Moses's life taking care of sheep for forty years was surely a bit boring and fairly predictable. His daily routine was probably not too exciting. However, that was all about to change because of a holy encounter in a holy place with a holy God.

One day, while Moses was minding his own business, he saw an unusual sight. A bush in the middle of nowhere was on fire. He paused and watched that bush, expecting it to burn up and die out. Perhaps he was also watching to make sure the fire didn't spread to any other dry vegetation close to it.

However, the bush did neither. It continued to burn, but not to burn up. Moses moved closer to get a better look. His daily routine could wait. Here was something different that might take some of his boredom away. His curiosity quickly turned to incredible awe and a holy fear as a voice spoke to him out of the fire. The man with a greater destiny than he could have ever imagined, heard his own name being called, *"Moses, Moses!" (Exodus 3:4)*

Moses responded with a frightened, "Here am I."

Then God spoke again, saying:

> *"Do not draw near this place. Take your sandals off your feet, for the place where you stand is holy ground." (Exodus 3:5)*

What was God saying?

A. This is not an ordinary day. This is not an ordinary bush. This is not an ordinary place. You are not an ordinary man, and I am not an ordinary God. This place and this bush have seen set apart for a special purpose, and you have also been called and set apart for a special purpose. Your days of boredom and routine are over. You will now become a shepherd to my people, Israel, and you will discover that I am not like any of the gods of Egypt that you were introduced to in your earlier life in the courts of Pharaoh.

B. Your old shoes speak of your old journey. That journey is over. Your shoes carry the dust of past wanderings and labor. It's time to take off the old and get ready for the new. Of course, shoes are still taken off in many cultures when one enters a home. This custom is based on the idea that the home is set apart from the contamination of the world. When you bring someone into your home, you are offering them protection and hospitality. In respect for the sanctity of your home, they will take off their shoes which they rightly feel carries the dust and contamination of the outside world. Moses was in close proximity to a place which God had set aside for Himself to encounter Moses. It was a temporary dwelling place for Him and as such, the ground around Him was holy or set apart.

So, let me summarize this point and say it again as clearly as possible. Holiness is not keeping a tradition or doing boring and traditional religious ceremonies. Holiness involves exciting, new and creative experiences, as Moses discovered in his special holy place.

2. Holiness Involves Being Encountered by God

God continued to talk with Moses:

"I am the God of your father—the God of Abraham, the God of Isaac, and the God of Jacob. And Moses hid his face, for he was afraid to look upon God."

We may not all have a "burning bush" experience like Moses, but the only way we can be truly holy is to have our own encounters with God. It's during these encounters that His own holiness rubs off on us, just like God's glory rubbed off on Moses when we was with God in the Holy Mountain.

At the moment, all I can say is "Wow!" as I feel the impact of a revelatory download from the Holy Spirit, which occurred when I finished writing the above verse on my computer.

This is what I just noticed for the first time in sixty years of reading Scripture: The first time Moses encountered the living God, He hid his own face, because He was afraid to look upon God. Sometime later, Moses was on the mountain with God and after interceding for Israel, and obtaining favor from God on their behalf, he begged for God to show him His glory.

In this encounter (Exodus 33:18-23), it was God, not Moses, who hid Moses's face to protect him from seeing the very face and the greater glory of God. Clearly, Moses was no longer afraid that he wasn't holy enough for God to accept him, as he had been earlier, and as so many Christians are today. Rather, every encounter with God gave him a hunger for even more—a hunger which overcame the fear of a Holy God.

I remember being told by a certain prophetic conference

speaker, who was blessed with a visit to Heaven, that he was afraid to be taken into the very presence of Jesus, and tried to resist the angels who escorted him into that holy place in Heaven. However, after looking into the eyes of Jesus and becoming overwhelmed with the depth and warmth of the love and power emanating from His eyes, he didn't want to ever leave. Once again he tried to resist the angels, but they pulled him away, knowing that if he stayed any longer, he would never want to return to earth.

But back to Moses on the Mountain of The Lord! To be holy, or "set apart for God" at that stage of his life, was not a burden for Moses. It was an awesome privilege. It meant that he had the honor and the incredible joy of an amazing encounter with the Living God, the God who was "set apart" from all other gods.

When Moses came down the mountain, he was not aware of the fact that His own face was glowing from spending time in God's glory. He was never allowed to see God's face in His full glory, but what he was exposed to was enough to illuminate his countenance like a high wattage light bulb, so that the people had to put a veil over his face, in order to be able to look in his direction.

The Burning Bush encounter with God was the first encounter for Moses after forty years in the wilderness, and as we mentioned earlier, it was in that encounter that the word, "holy" was first written into Scripture. By the time the five Books of Moses had been completed, the word, "holy" had been written in one hundred, fifty-eight different verses. In all the discussions and instructions for the wilderness tabernacle, known as "the tabernacle of Moses, almost every article, including the anointing oils, the clothes worn by Aaron and the priests, the

Ark of the Covenant and its contents, etc., were called holy, or set apart for God.

So far, we have seen that holiness was not associated with boring religion, but that it was associated with an exciting and powerful encounter with the living God. Clearly the word, "holy", had little to do with anything negative. It simply meant, "very special", and dedicated to a very special purpose and plan.

3. In the Holy Place, God Promised Great Blessing

"And The Lord said, 'I have surely seen the oppression of My people who are in Egypt, and have heard their cry because of their taskmasters, for I know their sorrows.

So I have come down to deliver them out of the hand of the Egyptians, and to bring them up from that land to a good and large land, to a land flowing with milk and honey, to the place of the Canaanites and the Hittites and the Amorites and the Perizzites and the Hivites and the Jebusites.

Now therefore, behold, the cry of the children of Israel has come to Me, and I have also seen the oppression with which the Egyptians oppress them.

Come now, therefore, and I will send you to Pharaoh that you may bring My people, the children of Israel, out of Egypt.'" (Exodus 3:7-10)

It was in this holy place, where Moses was required to remove his shoes, that God made some incredibly wonderful declarations, which we should all be able to apply to ourselves. This fact alone, should make us crave and passionately desire to enter into our own "holy place" with God. God declares several things in these powerful verses.

First, God says that He had "surely seen" the oppression Israel was experiencing. Wouldn't you love to hear God audibly declare to you that He has clearly seen what your enemy has been doing to you and that He was coming to your rescue. Where do I sign up for that holy encounter? My shoes are already off. I want to hear those words from His mouth about me.

Secondly, God says that He has heard their cry. So many people feel like their prayers are going unheard, because the answer still hasn't manifested. But in that holy place with God, he declares that He has heard our cry. What an amazing comfort to our souls.

Thirdly, God said that He knew their sorrows. Most people feel like there is no one who feels their pain. Others may try to give sympathy, but they remain uncomforted in their deep sorrow. Isn't it good to know that God can make it very clear in the time of our personal pain that He, Himself, has felt our pain and knows our sorrows.

Finally, God says that He has come down to take action. That action is two-fold. First, He promises to bring them OUT of their bondage. Then He promises to bring them INTO a wonderful place—a land flowing with milk and honey.

Reviewing again, we now have established that holiness is not a boring religious lifestyle, it does involve an exciting encounter with God, and in that encounter God reveals His love and concern for our problems and pain.

4. In the Holy Place God Speaks Purpose and Destiny into My Life

In verse 10, God gives Moses an awesome assignment, which is to go and stand before the Pharaoh and be used by God to bring His people out of their bondage and heavy labor and into their promised land. This call that God gave to Moses in his Holy Place encounter would make him one of the most famous leaders and lawgivers of all time. It would restore his original vision and empower him to do great exploits for God.

We know that Moses was so in need of inner healing that he had no confidence in himself to do anything that God was speaking to him about. Even though he was witnessing such an incredible miracle with God speaking out of the burning bush, Moses still objected and argued with God. Sadly, many people today are in the same boat and need someone to remind them that their past does not define their future. Rather, their past was schooling for ruling and training for reigning, even though they failed miserably in previous attempts to serve God. Remember, that both Moses and Peter—two of the greatest leaders in biblical history—failed badly when they tried to accomplish things in their own power.

The fact remains though, that God helped Moses overcome his insecurities and feelings of failure and he became the one person that God used to deliver His people and the only one we know of that ever had to veil his face because of the radiant glory of God shining from it.

So now, in addition to holiness not being boring and enabling us to have an exciting encounter with God, in which he promises great blessings to us, we are also called and commissioned to do great exploits for Him, giving us purpose, destiny and true fulfillment.

5. God Promises Favor and Prosperity in that Holy Encounter

Exodus 3 concludes with the promise that God would give Israel favor with the Egyptians and that they would plunder their former masters and take with them articles of gold, silver, clothing, etc. That sounds like pretty good news to me and it came while Moses was standing with his shoes off in that holy place of encounter with God.

So now we can add material prosperity promised along with all the other blessings of being in a holy place with God.

6. Miracles, Signs and Wonders are Found in the Holy Place Encounter with God

First God promised Moses that He would perform many great signs and wonders before Pharaoh, and then He taught Moses three signs that he would perform for the children of Israel and for Pharaoh. First, God turned Moses's shepherd's rod into a snake and then back into a rod. Then he made Moses's hand to become full of leprosy, before restoring it to normal. Finally, He told Moses how he would turn water into blood before Pharaoh in Egypt.

SUMMARY OF CURRENT FINDINGS

It sure sounds to me like being in the Holy Place with God is a pretty great and wonderful experience. It doesn't sound boring like typical religion portrays it. It sounds like a glorious adventure and it sounds like it's a place where I'm encouraged that my needs will get met in a wonderful way. It also sounds like in that Holy Place encounter, I will receive affirmation and a strategic assignment from God. Then I will be encouraged that God will give me favor and prosper me for the journey. Finally, I will be blessed with a demonstration of God's might power working through my own life and gifts.

Is it any wonder that our enemy doesn't want us to be drawn into that place of holiness or "set-apartness" with God? We must encourage ourselves and one another in The Lord to seek Him and His Holiness, pursuing one encounter after another, until, like Moses, our own faces shine and Isaiah 60:2 is fulfilled, so that "His glory will be seen upon us."

Immediately after writing this chapter on Moses and the burning bush, I read an article on THE ELIJAH LIST, submitted by prophets, Bob and Bonny Jones. The word they shared was to be released in their Shepherd's Rod, 2014. They mentioned the burning bush, a great baptism of fire and a highway of holiness.

Bob prophesied that there would be a greater emphasis on holiness than ever before. Bonny had a dream of a house on fire. Police were trying to keep people away from the house, but people came running and crossing the barricades to jump into the burning house. It was obviously speaking about the awesome fire of God in His church and it was drawing multitudes. Notice that people were not running away from this holy fire. Rather, like Moses they we moving closer to it and into it.

In Moses' time Jesus' blood had not yet been shed and Moses had to keep his distance from God, but today, we can come boldly into His presence. We can jump right into the fire and have our own "holy place" encounter with the God Who is a consuming fire.

Reading this article was a powerful confirmation to me that I was in Gods perfect will and had heard His voice concerning this subject. If holiness is to be a high priority, it seems to me that we need to understand it better, without the Medieval shadows darkening our interpretation of its application in the church and in the Kingdom of Heaven on the earth.

MOSES'S SUCCESSOR, JOSHUA, HAS A HOLY PLACE ENCOUNTER

Most Christians are not aware that there were two leaders who encountered God and were told to take of their shoes. Joshua was mentored by Moses for forty years and knew the ways of God. He was one of the two spies out of the twelve that brought a good report from their spy trip into the Promised Land, shortly after escaping Egypt. We also know that he loved the presence of God. We are told that when Moses left the tabernacle, which had been filled with God's glory, to speak to the people what God had spoken to him, that Joshua lingered there in the tabernacle.

But now, Moses was dead and Joshua was in charge. He did a great job of leading the people across the Jordan and getting them ready for battle. This included getting all the males circumcised at Gilgal. But Joshua did not yet have a strategy for taking Jericho.

Suddenly, as Joshua looked up, a "Man stood opposite him with his sword drawn in his hand." (Joshua 5:13)

This was no ordinary man. Joshua asked him if he was for or against them. The "Man" said "No, but as Commander of the army of The Lord I have now come. And Joshua fell on his face to the earth and worshiped, and said to Him, 'What does my Lord say to His servant?" (Joshua 5:14)

"Then the Commander of the Lord's army said to Joshua, 'Take your sandal off your foot, for the place where you stand is holy.' And Joshua did so." (Joshua 5:15)

IN THE HOLY PLACE ENCOUNTER, GOD CAN GIVE US STRATEGY TO WIN EVERY BATTLE

Joshua didn't need all the affirmation that Moses had needed, after his forty years in the wilderness tending sheep. Joshua certainly knew his calling and destiny. He had been mentored for forty years by one of the greatest leaders of all time. What Joshua needed was specific strategy for a specific battle. God gave him a "holy place" encounter to reveal a creative, out-of-the-box plan to bring down the mighty walls of Jericho.

We may be more prepared for our assignment than anyone else in the world, but we still need that "holy place" encounter to take advantage of the unfair advantage God has made available to us. Yes, Joshua might have still taken Jericho, but at what cost to his warriors? How often do we pay an unnecessary price to win our battles?

Once again, I believe it's easy to see that having a "Holy Place" encounter is not something to avoid, but something to pursue with passion. Of course, our motive should be intimacy with God—a desire to see His Glory and worship Him in Spirit and Truth. But the personal side-benefits seem to me to be rather incredible and certainly not something burdensome or too heavy to bear.

Chapter Four

The Joy of Holiness in Times of Restoration

There is one more powerful passage of Scripture that gives us a very refreshing view of holiness from the leaders of God's people during the time when God was restoring them to their possessions in their own Promised Land of Israel. Please read the following verses with your spiritual eyes wide open.

> *"So they read distinctly from the book, in the Law of God; and they gave the sense and helped them to understand the reading. And Nehemiah, who was the governor, Ezra the priest and scribe, and the Levites who taught the people said to all the people.* **This day is holy to The Lord** *your God; do not mourn nor weep.' For all the people wept, when they heard the words of the Law.*
>
> *Then he said to them, 'Go your way, eat the fat, drink the sweet, and send portions to those for whom nothing is prepared; for* **this day is holy to our Lord.** *Do not sorrow,*

for the joy of The Lord is your strength.' So the Levites quieted all the people, saying, **'Be still, for the day is holy;** *do not be grieved.' And all the people went their way to eat and drink, to send portions and rejoice greatly, because they understood the words that were declared to them." (Nehemiah 8:9-12)*

The setting for this passage is Jerusalem in the exciting time of restoration. The Jews, who had endured seventy years of bondage in Babylon, were rebuilding the walls of their great city. During their time of exile, they apparently did not have the privilege of hearing the words of their Sacred Writings.

But now, they were back in the land of their Fathers, and they could enjoy the privilege of hearing their own Holy Scriptures. Obviously, what they heard moved them deeply to tears. Nehemiah does not tell us the specific reasons for their profound emotional response, but we can imagine that they were made aware of the fact that, as a nation, they had seriously violated God's laws and were deserving of His judgment and wrath.

But the God-ordained leaders of this Restoration season, were quick to calm them and reassure them that God was with them and that they were not to be sad and sorrowful. Instead, God wanted them to rejoice and celebrate His mercy and grace toward them, in allowing them to return and rebuild the desolate city.

The most surprising thing, however, in this passage is the way Nehemiah, Ezra and the Levites related the joy and celebration concept with the fact that this was a "holy" day. Let's remind ourselves again that the word "holy" simply means set apart or special. What made it special and why were they not to be sad? Obviously, it was special because they finally got to listen to God's covenant word to His people. And the reason they were not to be sad, was that God wanted His encounters with us to be wonderful and joyful experiences.

The people were told three times in this one passage that the day was holy, and therefore they were not to weep or be sorrowful. Rather, they were to celebrate and give gifts to one another.

CHRISTMAS IS A HOLY DAY (OR HOLIDAY)

When we celebrate Christmas, we are keeping a Christian Holy Day. We have shortened the expression to "holiday," but it still means "Holy Day." It's a day for the joy of giving and receiving and we would never suggest that our children be sad and sober on that day. We want them to enjoy the gifts they have received as well as experience the joy of giving to others.

Even so, when we think of the word, "holy," we should never be thinking of sadness and sorrow. Rather, we should rejoice in the fact that God has given us this great gift of His holiness.

THE JOY OF THE LORD IS OUR STRENGTH

Most Christians have heard the above statement many times. Most Christians, however, are not aware of its context. The context was the fact that they were celebrating a Holy Day. The correct response was not to be sad and depressed or fearful. Rather, the people were told not to be sorrowful, because the joy of The Lord was their strength.

Obviously, God takes pleasure in giving us pleasure and joy. He also knows that to be strong for Him and to serve Him well, we need His joy. He provides that joy in the time He sets apart as "Holy Days." We will see more of this in the following pages.

THE HOLINESS MOVEMENT

As Divine Light began to penetrate the near opaque shadows of the Dark Ages in what is now known as the Reformation, Bibles began to be translated and published in the language of the people, thanks, in part, to the invention of the Gutenberg Press around AD 1450, and the courage of reformers who were willing to risk their lives to accomplish their reforms. As Bibles became more and more available in various European countries, including England, the impact of the Sacred Writings was profound and widespread.

Following the breakthrough restoration of such doctrines as Justification by Faith rather than works, and believer baptism rather than infant baptism, men like John Wesley began to pursue what the Bible referred to as Sanctification, a word that comes directly from the Greek word for Holiness. In the 1700's John and his brother, Charles, the hymn writer, along with many others, spent hours seeking for their own personal experiences with the Holy Spirit, in order that they could receive His touch and be transformed in their inner man. Their focus was on receiving what Jesus had from God while He walked on the earth, which enabled Him to live a sinless life.

The Wesley's and associates gave birth to the Methodists and Wesleyan denominations, which proclaimed a message of being separated from the world and holy unto God. They sought to continue what had been started back there in the eighteenth century.

Looking back through history, it is easy to see the cycles of revelation, revival, stagnation and decline. This, in my estimation, is what also took place in this movement.

The Holiness Movement had a powerful impact on the development of the Church in the Restoration process. Like the earlier Reformers such as Martin Luther, John Calvin, John Knox and others, the Wesleys did not bring in a full restoration of the early church. They added much and were at the cutting edge in their time, but God still had much more truth and experience to resurrect from the burial grounds of the former glorious church birthed through the early apostles and prophets of the first century.

What this Holiness Movement had right was the fact that our personal holiness would never be accomplished through our own individual effort and labor. It was not through the Dark Ages concept of penance, confession, Purgatory, indulgences, etc. No, this holiness could only be received as a free gift from God and it was a high value object to seek after diligently.

This holiness, according to Wesley, was an infusion of God's holiness and is supported by many Scriptures. One which says this well is II Peter 1:3,4.

> *"as His divine power has given to us all things that pertain to life and godliness, through the knowledge of Him who called us by glory and virtue, by which have been given to us exceedingly great and precious promises, that through these you may be partakers of the divine nature, having escaped the corruption that is in the world through lust."*

This passage contains many little nuggets that could be easily missed when reading it through the lens of our traditional concepts of holiness. For instance:

1. It is God's POWER that has given us everything we need to live a life pleasing to Him. This word, "power," is the Greek word "Dunamis," which means explosive power, like dynamite, a derivative of *dunamis*. God, Who uses His dynamic power to release His nature to us, is the same God who wants us to be unique and special (holy) like He is.

2. It's through the knowledge or "knowing" of Him that His power is transferred into our lives. This speaks to me of a life of intimacy, which is not a chore, but an incredible privilege.

3. "Exceedingly great" really means "the greatest" and is referring to God's promises which He has made to us in our intimacy with Him. It is the superlative of greatness and means there are no promises greater than the promises that He has made to us about giving us His very nature to enable us to live the true and holy Christian life.

4. These promises are also "precious," which means very costly and of high value. To provide this transfer of His very nature to us, it cost Jesus His life and His blood.

5. The word, "partaker," or *koino* in the Greek, also means "sharer" or "partner". Peter is declaring that we are actually partners or sharers of the very divine nature of God. That is truly incredible. And the practical application of this truth is very exciting to me. It means that if I pursue intimacy with God, I don't have to strive to be holy. Instead, His own nature is infused into my heart and soul and I find myself loving with His love and ministering with His power. As I recall my own unique testimony of God's visitation in my life as a nineteen-year-old, I am

once again moved to tears as I sit here and write. How vividly I remember God's love flowing through me to a person who was expressing anger towards me. I realized then, that God had done something supernatural, in that I was not reacting in my normal fleshly manner, but God, Himself, was loving through me.

6. "Having escaped the corruption that is in the world through lust," is another powerful and exciting statement. This holiness that God imparts to us when we pursue intimacy, is worth more than the most expensive life or health insurance policy. This infusion of God's nature is a wonderful insurance policy against the corruption that would destroy our lives without it. Like every natural living thing, our souls and bodies tend toward gradual deterioration and death. The carnal pleasures and sins we partake of have their destructive rewards and we find ourselves losing our health and our joy. But God's nature in us causes us to maintain and increase our joy and even our physical health.

GOING BEYOND THE HOLINESS MOVEMENT

The Holiness movement, under the leadership of John Wesley, was truly a movement that was taking the church in the right direction. However, like all the Reformation leaders, Wesley had his important contribution, but God would later add another dimension in the Restoration process.

What God wants to add to our understanding of holiness in our generation is that holiness, or "set-apartness" includes the supernatural, miraculous, signs and wonders aspect. Somehow, we find it easy to ascribe that aspect of "set-apartness" to God, but we find it more difficult to assign that aspect to us, who are called to "be holy as God is holy."

I want to make a bold statement here that I believe with all my heart.

Unless we display the power of God along with the love of God, we are not truly "Holy as He is holy."

God is set apart from other gods because of His power and His love that flows out of Him. We must be set apart from other people on the earth because of His power and His love flowing through us.

Once again, we must be reminded that this holiness comes through intimacy and is not of our own works or self-discipline. It comes from Him and He gets the glory.

INTIMACY

When we talk about intimacy, some of us may feel a little burdened with responsibility to spend more time in prayer, Bible reading, soaking, etc. We think in previous religious paradigms of guilt and obligation.

Instead, let's think about the glorious joys and privileges of intimacy. Think of the glorious fact that Jesus has set aside time for us. He wants to be there to listen to our heart's cries and desires. He wants to share His secrets with us and tell us how important we are to Him and His Kingdom. Think about the fact that natural intimacy leads to wonderful and ecstatic feelings of love and being loved. Yes, think about it! And then realize that intimacy with God—Father, Son and Holy Spirit—has to be so incredibly more wonderful than any earthly intimacy.

It's not a burden to pursue intimacy. Rather, it's an open door, an exciting opportunity, an incredible adventure and the most fulfilling experience we can imagine.

Therefore, pursuing holiness is an off-the-charts glorious opportunity to discover the love, joy and peace that the whole world is hungry for. What a wonderful and awesome God we serve! He is a God Who offers us everything we could ever desire and more.

It's time now to change the subject slightly and take a look at the purpose and blessings of one of the Holy Days that God gave us. Let's take a fresh and uplifting view of the Sabbath.

Chapter Five

The Precious Gifts of the Sabbath and the First Day

Having just discussed the spirit of joy attached to the Holy Day celebrated in the book of Nehemiah, we will now tackle the very controversial subject of the purpose and appropriate manner of keeping the Sabbath in a Restoration, New Testament Church setting. Like holiness, our understanding of the Sabbath is still very foggy, obscured by the lingering shadows of the Dark Ages and the teachings of the Scribes and Pharisees of Bible times.

Jesus Reveals the Purpose of the Sabbath

Because the nation of Israel rejected deeper intimacy with God, in favor of religious rules, God often did not give them the reasons for the laws they were to keep. For instance, many of the laws handed down by Moses were designed to keep the people healthy, but they didn't necessarily understand that. The book,

None of These Diseases, written by David E. McMillen, a medical doctor, pointed out how so many of the laws, given through Moses, protected God's people from the diseases afflicting Egypt and other nations at that time.

These diseases included certain cancers, leprosy and others. It is one of the proofs of the supernatural wisdom given to Israel through Moses. It predated the scientific medical knowledge by thousands of years.

The point, which we are making here, is that God gave them rules without understanding in the Old Covenant relationship. However, Jesus came to bring in a New Covenant—one in which He would give us a heart to know Him in an intimate way. (Ezekiel 36:26,27, Jeremiah 31:31-34, II Corinthians 3:6-18)

Jesus made many comments on the Sabbath, revealing the fact that the Scribes and Pharisees had no idea why God had given it to them. They were certainly under the Old Covenant condition of religion without relationship.

Here is the Scripture where Jesus gives us the greatest key to understanding the purpose and power of the Sabbath:

"And He said to them, 'The Sabbath was made for man, and not man for the Sabbath. Therefore the Son of Man is also Lord of the Sabbath.'" (Mark 2:27,28)

Jesus was revealing that the religious leaders had gotten so intense in their pursuit of keeping the Sabbath "holy" to The Lord, that they had made the Sabbath more important than the people. They had the mindset that God was more concerned with them keeping the Sabbath than with them loving His people.

But Jesus revealed something even more important to us:

He made the Sabbath for us—not for Himself. Religious leaders in the Kingdom of God still miss this point. Even those who call Sunday the "New Sabbath" miss the point. He made the Sabbath for us—not for Himself.

My Newest Insight on the Sabbath —I Think You'll Like It!!!

Based on the Mark 2:27 passage, we know that God made the Sabbath for us. How is that true and what does the Sabbath do for us?

The obvious answer is that our bodies need a break from normal labor. In Jesus' time, there were few people who sat at desks all day. Most did physical work and their bodies needed rest. We have always understood that.

But something else dropped into my spirit recently. Here it is:

If the people were not allowed to do normal work on the Sabbath, what would they do with their time? If you lived before the days of electronic gadgets, TV, movies and recorded music, what would you do with your time on a day when you weren't allowed to do any productive work?

You would spend time in communication with your family and with God. You would have your weekly "Family Day." You would listen to each other's hearts and share stories from your past. You would talk about your ancestors and their experiences with God. You would really get to know one another on a more intimate level, while your body was resting from six days of toil. In addition, you would set aside time for worshipping the God that blessed you with a day of rest.

You see, people are competitive and history reveals, as does God's Word, that the Jewish people were destined to be blessed and prosperous on the earth. They have something, I think, in their DNA that enables them to get ahead. With that inner drive to succeed, it's no wonder that God commanded them all to stop their work for one day of the week. It was to be a "holy day" or "holiday." They could enjoy their families and neighbors without worrying that someone else would get ahead of them in business, etc.

What a blessing the Sabbath really was and still is! The Jews didn't understand its purpose, but they enjoyed its fruit. As we shall see, we can also participate in that fruit today if we learn to appropriately apply its principles and New Covenant understanding.

THE SABBATH VS. THE FIRST DAY OF THE WEEK

A number of Christian denominations as well as Messianic Jews have made an issue of how important it is to keep the Sabbath rather than making Sunday their "day of worship." Rather than argue theologically from research into the Hebrew and Greek Scriptures as well as Church History, I want to offer a little revelatory insight, combined with a little "horse sense" based on what Jesus said and did.

I find it misses the whole point to ask which day God wants us to set aside for worship. That is still Old Covenant thinking to me. Every single day should be set aside for worship. Part of our problem is that we still call a building "the church." We say that we "go to church on Sunday." But if we are living stones of the church, we are the church and we are always in church.

God inhabits our praises and thus, as long as we keep praising Him, we are His Tabernacle and Temple.

Of course, I'm not saying that we don't need to gather as part of the Body of Christ on a regular day. I think we could actually do that every day, like the early church did, and still please God. It's always about our hearts, in God's eyes, not the externals. He looks for those whose pure hearts worship Him in Spirit and Truth, which means those who are intimate with Him, who is the Way, the Truth and the Life, and have His Spirit directing them and assisting them in worship.

The Sabbath was made for man, so the primary purpose of the Sabbath was not the gathering for worship, but for man to rest and be refreshed. That would involve being in God's presence as well as fellowship with others, but the Sabbath was not about a meeting—it was about rest. The long discussion in the Book of Hebrews about the Sabbath is mainly about entering into a rest in God's presence.

What about Sunday, or as it is more correctly called, the first day of the week? Does it replace the Sabbath for Christians? No! It is not the Christian Sabbath. God did not ever replace the Sabbath. He only gave it new meaning and gave us more understanding of its purpose. The word, "Sabbath" means seventh, and thus cannot be the seventh and the first day at the same time.

So why do Christian churches meet mostly on Sunday? I believe there is a good reason to do that and we will try to make it as clear as possible. The reason we do it is not because God told us to, because He really didn't. The reason we do it is because we can give God the first fruits of our week and seek first His Kingdom.

As you will discover, if you have the courage to keep reading, I believe that both the Sabbath and the First Day have a significant role to play in the life of every believer. We will first talk about the historical perspective and then the prophetic perspective. Then we will make an attempt to make some practical applications, so that this will not just become another theological football to toss around and argue about.

1. The Historical Perspective of the Sabbath

As we shall quickly see, the major events in history are highlighted by the Sabbath and the First Day when we look at the historical and prophetic aspects of these days. God has given us beautiful reminders of His love and of His awesome plans for His people. Remember that His plans for us are that we would have a future and a hope.

The Sabbath looks back to where it all began for us—The Creation. Yes, it represents the seventh day—the day God rested from His work, but a little common sense tells us to focus a lot more on what He was resting from. We should ask the question here: Was God tired? I think not! When it says, He rested, it means He stopped what He had been doing because He was finished.

I believe we should remember the Sabbath for what God did on the six days before He rested.

Here's something else that just floated into my mind: Shouldn't we use the Sabbath to look back on the past week and reflect on how much we were able to accomplish by the grace of God? Shouldn't it be a time to celebrate the creativity that God put into our spirit when He made us in the image of Himself, the great Creator?

I am very convinced in my own heart and soul that we can make the Sabbath a great day of joy and celebration like they did in the days of Nehemiah when they read the law of God to the former exiles and called it a holy day. I think we could really profit in our inner soul if we took time to rejoice in the fact that God, the Creator, was creating through us and producing new things in our world. Like God, we should be able to look back at each day and say, "Wow! That was good!"

In addition, it might be a good time to focus with our children on the creation itself. Studying about all the things that God created in the context of how glorious a world He made would make the Sabbath very meaningful. We can tell our children that because God finished His amazing creation, we can have awesome adventures discovering the amazing varieties of every field of natural science, including geography, geology, biology, zoology, botany, and so many more.

2. The Historical Perspective of the First Day

As every Christian is aware, our Savior was resurrected from the dead on the first day of the week. Next, He appeared to Mary and His disciples on the first day of the week. Then He appeared again to them, with Thomas present on the first day of the next week.

It is surely obvious to every reader that the Resurrection of Jesus is the most important historical event for a Christian. Without the Resurrection, we are still in our sins. I Corinthians 15 is devoted almost entirely to the great importance of the Resurrection. So for us, it is fitting to celebrate this incredibly important event once a week. It is a reminder that we are not in a religion of rules and rituals. We are in a relationship with a living God, One Who lives within us and through us.

Obviously, the Resurrection was preceded by the Crucifixion. The two events are inseparable. What makes the Resurrection so exciting is that it reversed the sorrow and pain of the Crucifixion from just days earlier. Thus the Resurrection is a reminder that when things look their worst, God has a way of turning the biggest defeats into His greatest victories.

Thus, in both of these celebrations—the Sabbath and the First Day—the day of celebration looks back to the previous days and rejoices in the completion and the finished work of both events. The Creation was completed, enabling the Creator to rest from His work, and the the work of Jesus was completed (His life and His death), so that He could now be endowed with Resurrection Life, which He could breathe into His disciples in John 20:22.

The Jews were given several annual feasts to celebrate and remember what God had done for them. Most of these were joyful feasts and causes for great celebrations and parties. God knows our need to have special events to look forward to and to give us breaks from the routine and mundane. Thus, we have the privilege of celebrating both the Sabbath and the First Day, based on major events in human history.

3. The Prophetic Perspective of the Sabbath

If you have a significantly different end-times or eschatological view, you may not agree with this or the next topic (#4). But if you believe that Revelation 20:1-6 is literal, you will be excited about this truth.

We are told in the above passage that Satan will be bound for 1000 years and the believers will rule and reign with Christ for those thousand years. Since the Bible tells us that one day is like a thousand years to God and a thousand years like a day (II Peter 3:8), and we have seen six of those thousand-year days go by, many scholars believe that we are very close to the seventh thousand-year day, which will be a thousand-year day of rest. After all, when the devil is bound and cast into the bottomless pit for a thousand years, we will have a very special rest from temptation and sin.

Thus, when we celebrate the Sabbath, we can look both back to Creation and forward to the thousand-year day of rest. It makes the Sabbath a lot more exciting and meaningful. After all, what is so exciting about God resting? Not much really, unless we focus on what He had first accomplished in creating everything, including us, as well as what He has planned for us. The Nation of Israel had almost no idea why God wanted them to keep the Sabbath, but they kept it religiously. Now God has given us far greater understanding and we can celebrate it with great excitement because we know what God has done for us and what He will do for us in the future.

4. The Prophetic Perspective of the First Day

The first day of the week represents a brand new beginning. It's the beginning of a new week, which represents the fact that the old week is over.

Whereas the Sabbath looks forward to the thousand-year Millennium Rest, the First Day looks forward to the New Heavens and New Earth, which follows the Millennium Rest.

We could go to many Scriptures which talk about God doing a "new thing." You will find them in Isaiah 42, 43 and 44, as well as many other prophetic passages. But we find the most specific and applicable verses in the book of Revelation. Here's what I'm talking about:

> *Now I saw a new heaven and a new earth, for the first heaven and the first earth had passed away. Also there was no more sea. Then I, John, saw the holy city, New Jerusalem, coming down out of heaven from God, prepared as a bride adorned for her husband.*
>
> *And I heard a loud voice from heaven saying, "Behold, the tabernacle of God is with men, and He will dwell with them, and they shall be His people. God Himself will be with them and be their God.*
>
> *And God will wipe away every tear from their eyes; there shall be no more death, nor sorrow, nor crying. There shall be no more pain, for the former things have passed away."*
>
> *Then He who sat on the throne said, "Behold, I make all things new." And He said to me, "Write, for these words are true and faithful." (Revelation 21:1-5)*

The above passage certainly gives us a lot to think about and celebrate as we look forward to God wiping every tear from our eyes. Those who still struggle with physical pain from arthritis or cancer, etc., surely have a great sense of anticipation of this final stage of history (His story).

Notice how many times God uses the word "new" in the passage, and how it ends with the declaration, "Behold, I make all things new." We should certainly be in a mood to celebrate on the First Day when we think of what we have to look forward to, while at the same time we realize that it is all because of what we can look back upon.

Most of us enjoy the excitement of moving into a new house, especially if it's one we've dreamed of and built to our own specifications. It is particularly exciting if our previous home had serious problems and limitations.

I remember the joy of moving into the house we have now lived in for nine years. For the previous five years we had lived with our two youngest sons in an RV as we travelled in ministry around the USA and Canada. Finally, after five years in very tight living quarters, we had space and comfort as God supplied furniture and beds for all of us in a nice and roomy brand new house. What a joy that was, even though God had given us grace for five years to live in a very small space.

Now, imagine your life in this age being like living in a small boxcar with no furniture but knowing that shortly you will be moving into your dream home in the New Jerusalem. Imagine a home where there was no spending limit and every imaginable luxury was available. Imagine a home in which God's glory was always present and love, joy and peace flowed out of every glowing particle in the floor, walls, ceiling and its very atmosphere.

That would be a great thing to think about on the First Day. Why not take time to make a "wish list" for your Heavenly home in the New Jerusalem? God won't mind at all! In fact, I imagine He's wondering why you haven't done it yet. I believe He wants us to to excited about our future with Him. He knows it will help us to get through some pretty rough days down here in this present age.

Quick Summary

Let's review what we've just discussed. Both the Sabbath and the First Day have special importance to a Christian.

The Sabbath looks back on the wonders of Creation and looks forward to the joys of the Millennium.

The First Day looks back on the Crucifixion and the Resurrection and looks forward to the New Heaven and the New Earth.

Next we will see God's wisdom in the order of these days of celebration.

THE SABBATH, THE FIRST DAY AND THE FIRST FRUITS PRINCIPLE

We know that throughout the Old Testament, God revealed His desire and legal requirement that His people give Him the first fruits of all their goods. He even told them that their first born child belonged to Him. However, He allowed them to substitute an animal for their child and were allowed to keep their child. They were to do this as a reminder that everything they had came from God and that this first fruits principle should apply to everything.

The tithe was part of this principle. Ten percent of their income was to be given to God as a reminder that it all came from Him. They were to give the first ten percent, not the last.

We know that Jesus came to fulfill the Old Covenant and the Law, but not to destroy it. He certainly validated the First Fruits principle when He told His disciples in Matthew 6:33, to seek first the Kingdom of Heaven and all the things that the Gentiles seek would be added unto them. This is, of course, not the only New Testament reference to first fruits. You can find a number of them revealing that Jesus was Himself the First Fruits of God's new covenant with man.

So how does the Sabbath and the First Day relate to this principle?

The Sabbath is the last day of the week. It is the day that follows six days of labor. It is the day that God gave to man. It was man's day to rest from his labor, following the example of God who rested from His labor. God rested, not because He was tired, as we mentioned earlier, but because He was finished His work, and He knew that man would be tired after six days of labor.

The First Day, however, which follows the Seventh Day or Sabbath, is the day in which a working man will have the most energy or strength after a whole day of rest. The First Day is the first fruits of a brand new week. For us, who are Christians, it is the day that we give to God to serve Him, instead of ourselves.

Let's do the math:

There are 168 hours in a week. A tithe, or tenth, of these hours would be 16.8 hours. People normally sleep between seven and eight hours of each day. That leaves between sixteen and seventeen hours that a person is awake in any given day.

Therefore, if we subtract the hours we sleep on the First Day, it leaves us with roughly the tithe of the hours of our week to give completely to God. Then we have the next five days to work for ourselves and our families, and after those five days of working for ourselves, we can enjoy the Sabbath rest to get refreshed for the new week.

Since we are no longer under the law, we do not advocate any legalistic adherence to the above principle. It can however, be a guideline and a guiding light in the way we live our lives.

GETTING PRACTICAL

In addition to some thoughts already shared, let's make some additional suggestions to apply the principles discussed above. I think the best suggestions will come from asking ourselves some pointed questions. Here are a few:

Questions

1. How much quality time am I spending with family members and others that are very important to me? Do I really know them and do they really know me? Do I take time to interact on a deep heart-to-heart level? Do I take time off from my normal routine and electronic gadgets to look them in the eye and ask them the important questions that let them know that they are important to me?
2. Have I been under stress because I seldom take time to forget the pressures of my work and just focus on relationships and a change of scenery? Am I needing to take medications to sleep, handle pain, or cope with other physical ailments just because I have too much stress in my life?
3. Do I enjoy God's creation and teach my children or others about God's amazing creativity and natural science?
4. Do I have a hard time saying no to the urgent when there is something actually more important that needs my attention?
5. Have I found my church life becoming a matter of routine

or obligation? Or do I get excited about celebrating the historical and prophetic aspects of my relationship with God?

6. Do I feel too tired to spend time in worship or ministry because of exhaustion and stress?

7. Do I and my family love to talk about Heaven, angels, and what it will be like to be free from temptation, pain and sorrow?

8. Do I find myself complaining more than praising God for what He has done?

9. Do I hate thinking about these questions, because I feel like a failure?

10. Do I want to see more practical fruit in my life?

Suggestions

Based on how you answered these questions, you might want to consider some of these suggestions.

1. Ask God for wisdom for your particular situation to prioritize your time to deepen relationships with Him, with your family and other people close to you.

2. Start small with modest changes in your schedule that will be workable in your particular lifestyle. Biting off too much may cause you to give up on the whole thing.

3. Make a list of priorities in your life and think about how you will handle requests from people that will take you away from what is most important.

4. Ask your spouse and children and other important people in your life if they feel like they would want more quality

time with you and ask them for suggestions about what
that would look like.

5. Ask God how you could serve Him, especially on the
First Day, after you have had some rest, if you are able
to actually rest on the Sabbath. Gathering as the church
is a great start, but perhaps there are other ways that you
and your family could put first His Kingdom. Often
there are opportunities to visit lonely people in hospitals,
nursing homes, jails, etc. There are people who could use
a prophetic word or a prayer for healing or other needed
miracles in their lives. This could even be done over the
phone or by e-mail or social networks. You may find this
very addictive as you experience the miracle power of God
flowing through your life.

6. You may need to cut down on your work load, or at least
limit the hours you spend away from your family, so you
can focus on your priorities?

7. Be careful not to make this a religious thing. Rather, make
it fun and exciting for yourself and your family. Just try
to be creatively different than before and different than
what you do on the five working days of the week.

8. Share this chapter with others who may be interested in
making changes with you, so you can have some support
and enjoy a little more fun and variety in your adventures
by doing things together as a family. Feel free to photo-
copy any part of this book.

9. Remember, both the Sabbath and the First Day are days
to celebrate and have a God-party. Don't let the shadows
of the Dark Ages hover over your season of celebration.

10. Don't forget that giving our first fruits to God on the First

Day is not a burdensome assignment. It's a celebration of the opportunity to watch Him work through you. It's a different kind of labor than what you do for a living. It is a great adventure if you allow yourself the paradigm shift.

QUICK SUMMARY

The New Covenant is a celebration of freedom from the law and freedom to be a son or daughter of the King of kings. We want to apply that to every doctrine and New Testament practice, so we don't become another branch of the "Church of the Self-righteous."

It was clearly because of God's love for His people that He gave them the Sabbath. It kept them healthy and gave them a richer life. Jesus and the Apostles never told us to celebrate the First Day, but there is evidence that they connected for fellowship on that day, and we know that the First Day was the day that the disciples found the empty tomb.

I know people with a strong religious persuasion about the Sabbath will argue with my conclusions and try to prove me wrong from their leaders' research. I'm finished arguing about it from a scholarly point of view. Rather, I see so clearly that we have something to celebrate on both special days and the more we can party with the Father, Son and Holy Spirit, the happier our lives will be.

To sum it up, let's remember that the Sabbath is still the Sabbath. We just understand more about its purpose and it's blessing. It is significant because we can celebrate God's creativity and we can get excited about the coming Millennium. The First Day is still the First Day and it has its own meaning and significance to us as Christians who believe in the Resurrection and the New Heaven and the New Earth.

So let's enjoy the great blessings of God's provision and wisdom and stop arguing about which day God has set apart. You can't go wrong by celebrating His goodness on both days.

The basic principles however are simply this:

Work for your personal needs on Day Two through Day Six. Rest and change your routine on the Sabbath, taking time for fellowship with God and family, remembering the creation and the coming Millennium. Then, with renewed strength and energy, celebrate the Resurrection and the New Heavens and New Earth on the First Day, taking extra time to use your spiritual gifts to bless His Kingdom. May God give us all wisdom to follow the wise and beautiful patterns He gave us to follow with the freedom to follow the leading of the Holy Spirit when someone needs a helping hand on the Sabbath.

Chapter Six

Communion —
What We've Been Missing

How many theological arguments have raged over the sacrament of communion throughout the centuries since the days of the early church? No one knows the answer, of course, but whatever the number might be, it's certainly far too many. Theologians have fought over the meaning of words like "is" while seldom, if ever. noticing some of the more obvious blessings and applications of the Lord's Supper.

As we have seen with The Sabbath, we will see also with Communion, that there is a historical aspect—but much more than we normally celebrate—and there is a prophetic aspect, which we have missed almost completely.

As we mentioned in the first chapter, Dark Ages thinking has dominated the way we look at Communion. The focus was always on the pain and suffering of Jesus, and how grateful we should be, and how willing we should also be to suffer for Him. Of course, Evangelicals have focused more on the gift of Salvation and the power of the blood to cleanse us from sin, but the Church as a whole has missed a very important meaning and application of Communion.

We hope to clearly demonstrate in this chapter that this failure to truly understand what Jesus gave us in Communion has not only deprived us of a blessing God intended us to have, but it has deprived Jesus of the honor and glory and fruitfulness that He deserves from His church.

THE HISTORICAL ASPECTS OF COMMUNION

Jesus was about to die so that all who believed in Him might live. He spent some precious hours with His disciples, knowing that they would be totally devastated by His departure. He wanted to give them a visual aid to help them remember the most important things that He had to teach them after they recovered from the shock of His death, resurrection and ascension.

So, as was His style, He used a natural situation to illustrate a spiritual truth. He took the bread and the wine and passed them out while making statements that they would not immediately understand. However, He commanded them to repeat the process frequently after His departure, and He knew that the Holy Spirit would give them greater understanding of what He was saying to them.

As we all know, He said, "This is my body, which is broken for you. Do this in remembrance of Me." Then He declared, "This cup is the New Covenant in My blood." (I Corinthians 11:24,25) These words have been read millions of times in churches around the world, but seldom have been totally understood.

Typical Interpretation:

We usually are reminded of how much Jesus suffered when His body was "broken." Then we are reminded that His blood was shed to forgive our sins. After that we are exhorted to examine ourselves to make sure we don't have any unconfessed sin, lest we get sick and die for "eating unworthily." For the most part, there is nothing wrong with the above, and it is a good thing to realize the price Jesus paid for our Salvation, and of course, it's a good thing to examine our hearts before The Lord.

A MORE POWERFUL APPLICATION OF COMMUNION

The fact is, however, that when Jesus said, "This is My body, which is broken for you," He really wasn't talking about the pain and suffering He would experience. The word for "broken" was the word consistently used for breaking break together. It simply meant the dividing up of a loaf among them, where each would have his piece to eat. Jesus was clearly saying, "I am dividing up My body among you, My disciples."

To understand what Jesus was saying, we need to examine the context of Paul's teaching on Communion, and use a little common sense to put two and two together and figure out the sum.

When this insight began to break through my traditional mindset on this subject, I was reading in I Corinthians 10. Paul's main teaching on Communion follows in chapter 11. That is the portion usually quoted in Communion services. Then chapter 12 is a long and detailed discussion about spiritual gifts and the body of Christ, where different gifts and ministries give us different functions in the body.

Here is the portion that radically adjusted my understanding of Communion:

"The cup of blessing, which we bless, is it not the communion of the blood of Christ? The bread which we break, is it not the communion of the body of Christ? For we, though many, are one bread and one body, for we all partake of that one bread." (I Corinthians 10:16,17)

It should be noted here that the word communion used here actually means sharing. So drinking from the cup is sharing the blood of Christ and eating the bread is the sharing of the body of Christ. When we think of the word, communion, we are usually either thinking of fellowship with Jesus and other believers or just thinking of the ceremony with the bread and wine. But if we call it sharing, then we are receiving something together and there is a sense of interdependence that goes along with it. This is a much deeper, or more involved, concept than fellowship.

What really hit me in this passage was the fact that Paul said, we are "one bread." Before that, I had thought, as others did, that the bread was Jesus' body, but I never thought that we were also the bread ourselves. If we are one bread and one body, then there is more here than what we have taught and been taught for centuries.

As we just mentioned, Chapter 12 talks about the body of Christ, right after Paul's more detailed teaching on communion. In addition, chapter 12 talks about different types of spiritual gifts. Things were beginning to take shape in my understanding.

When Jesus said He was dividing up His body among the disciples, He was talking about the spiritual gifts that Paul said the Holy Spirit divided up in the body, so that the body could function. (I Corinthians 12:4-11)

LET'S THINK ABOUT THE BODY OF CHRIST

Jesus had a normal human body as a man. What did He do with His body? Why did He need a body on the earth? Why do we have bodies? What do we do with them?

I asked these questions in a church in Yorkton, Saskatchewan, and I got the answer from a worship leader there that I love to quote. He said, "You need a body so you can do stuff."

Jesus needed a body so He could do stuff here on the earth. We also have bodies so we can do stuff here on the earth. And Jesus still needs a body on the earth so He can still "DO STUFF."

We must remember that JESUS DID NOT GIVE US GIFTS SO WE COULD HAVE A MINISTRY AND FEEL IMPORTANT. Yes, He wants us to feel important to Him and He wants us to have a ministry, but that's not why He gave us the gifts primarily.

JESUS GAVE US GIFTS SO HIS BODY WOULD HAVE THE POWER AND ABILITY TO DO STUFF ON THE EARTH, JUST LIKE HE DID WHEN HE HAD HIS INDIVIDUAL BODY TO WORK THROUGH.

Communion then, is not just a solemn remembrance of Jesus' pain and suffering. I don't really think He needs our sympathy or desires it. He is doing just fine at the right hand of His Father in Heaven. What make Him sad is the fact that we don't fulfill our potential, when we don't utilize the powerful gifts and callings that He has given to every believer, which is symbolized by the bread that is shared in our Communion services.

Rather than just spending time feeling Jesus' pain for us, SHARING THE BREAD SHOULD REALLY BE A CELEBRATION OF THE FACT THAT THROUGH HIS DEATH AND RESURRECTION, HE TRANSFERRED HIS GIFTS AND MINISTRIES TO US, SO THAT WE COULD BE HIS BODY ON THE EARTH, AND SO THAT HE COULD DO STUFF THROUGH US.

It is an interesting fact that, although Jesus supernaturally appeared to the disciples and as many as five hundred others, after his resurrection, we have no record of Jesus, Himself, healing anyone or performing any miracles. He did tell the disciples where to cast their nets, but He let them do the work so they could have some fish to eat.

When you break pieces from a loaf, there are many rough and jagged edges, but when you put them back together, like a jigsaw puzzle, they reform that beautiful loaf with smooth and shiny skin and no rough edges. However, if we all take pride in who we are and refuse to connect with other pieces of the loaf, we present some really jagged edges to those we try to minister to.

And Now—the Wine

But what about the cup of wine, which represents the blood? Is there more to this element of Communion than just being thankful for His blood which cleanses us from sin. (I Peter 1:18,19) That is an incredible gift to us, but is there more that we have been missing? When Jesus said, "This cup is the New Covenant in My blood." what was He referring to?

Of course, blood has cleansing and covering properties. It was also the means of protection from the angel of death in Exodus and it represented the sacrifice that Jesus paid to forgive our sins. It was also said that life itself is in the blood of any creature. Scientifically, this is true, as the blood carries the oxygen, which keeps the cells of the body alive.

Thus we know that Jesus sacrificed His blood (His physical life) to give us spiritual life. That is the salvation and redemption part that we commemorate in communion. But how does the concept of the life giving properties of the blood relate to the concept of the body and bread, which we have been discussing?

Based on a study of several verses about the New Covenant, I believe that drinking from the cup also represents receiving an impartation or filling of the Spirit of Life—the Holy Spirit. And just as the blood flows to the organs and cells of the body, bringing the breath of life to it, so the Holy Spirit, which also means, "Holy Breath," was given to flow through His body and bring life to every member of His body. The oxygen in the blood empowers every cell to do what it's called to do. Without that oxygen, the cell would die and the whole body would die.

Just as we plug in different electrical appliances to the same wall socket and get different results, so we have the same Holy Spirit flowing through us, but we manifest different gifts. A toaster makes toast, but a vacuum cleaner, sucks up the dirt in the carpet when plugged into the same source of power.

Even so, the eyes use the oxygen to see, while the ears use the oxygen to hear. The liver and kidneys, heart and lungs all have different applications for the same source of power. But in the body of Christ, the same source of life and power produces faith in one person, miracles in another, prophecy in another, words of knowledge in another, wisdom in another, healing in another, discerning of spirits in another, tongues and/or interpretation of tongues in another. The same source of power also manifests in apostolic gifts in one, prophetic, evangelistic, pastoral and teaching in others. But we all drink from the same source, the life-giving Holy Spirit of God, which flows like wine, water or blood into every part of His body, His Bride, His church.

The New Covenant is in the blood, according to Jesus. The Word tells us that God is writing His New Covenant in our hearts, (Jeremiah 31:33, Ezekiel 36:26,27) making us soft and tender towards His leading in our lives. We know that this is what the Holy Spirit does. He teaches us the ways and thoughts of God and gives us the desire to love and serve Him.

We could discuss and exegete a multitude of passages on the Holy Spirit and spiritual gifts. However, that would fill many more books. For the purposes of this book, we just want to simply declare that the clear teaching of Paul in I Corinthians leads us to believe that Communion should be a time of great celebration and thankfulness to God for everything He has done for us on the cross, and especially for the great and awesome privilege of being His body here on the earth.

It is true that we are told to remember the Lord's death and not treat the "Lord's Supper" with disrespect, but as we have discovered, the death He suffered enabled us to have life, and to have it more abundantly. What makes Jesus happy and gives Him the the reward He deserves is not that we feel sad for Him, but that we actually become His body, accepting His gifts and ministries and work together as one body to build His Kingdom and prepare the nations for His return.

The tone of Paul's instruction concerning Communion may seem somber and serious, but we must remember that He was writing to a church that had many problems related to their heart attitudes and behaviors. They were not valuing what Jesus had done for them. Some of them were drunk and behaving badly while taking communion.

One of Paul's warnings was actually about "not discerning the Lord's body." Paul could have meant by this that they were not realizing that they had a responsibility as a part of the body of Christ to function soberly in that role that the Holy Spirit had given them. It could also mean that they were not honoring Jesus for the sacrifice He had made for them and they were not honoring the other members of His body that they were connected to.

Going back to the actual first Communion in the Upper Room, I believe we can feel the heart of Jesus in the statements that He made. As I visualize Him saying, "This is My body, which is divided up for you," I can feel His love and desire for their success flowing to them. The words, "for you" have great importance here. If He was actually talking about His work and ministry, rather than just His physical body suffering harm, then when He said, "for you" He was telling them that He was giving them something so wonderful and powerful that it was beyond their ability to comprehend.

What He was saying then was really the fact that they were going to do all the things that He had done and even more. This is what He had just told them as recorded in John 14:12. And now He was giving them a visual aid to remember His promise to them. For just as He had done His work through a physical body, they would be doing His work on earth through His new physical body, as long as they worked together and functioned as one.

NEW UNDERSTANDING

As I am writing this part of the chapter, I am experiencing an awareness of God's presence on me and I have a deep assurance that He is imparting even more understanding on this subject than I've ever had before. Here's what I am beginning to understand in a greater measure:

Communion (or sharing His body and blood) was really just a visual aid to remember all that He had told them in John 14-17. This special talk with the twelve happened just before He was arrested in the garden, where Judas betrayed Him to His enemies. So what had Jesus been teaching them in those chapters?

He had told them many things, including the following:

1. He talked first about their reward in Heaven in John 14. This makes perfect sense. They needed a long-term positive vision and awareness of a great and eternal destiny to prepare them to handle some very negative experiences, which would follow immediately.
2. Then Jesus told them that they would do the same things that He had done (John 14:12) and even greater things would they do. He was now bringing vision to the near future and giving them something to get excited about, which would also help them deal with the hard things that were facing them.
3. He told them next that He would send The Comforter, the Holy Spirit. They would not be left alone to sorrow and grieve. Then He told them many things that the Holy Spirit would do for them. This filled up most of the next three chapters.

4. In John 15, Jesus talked about the Vine and the branches and how important it was for them to abide and stay connected to Him. He was not yet using the "body" symbolism, but something simpler for them to understand. The branches die if they disconnect from the vine. His promise to them, however, was that if they stayed connected to Him, they would bring forth much fruit.

5. Jesus continued His teaching in John 15 by saying that He was giving them His joy, so their joy could be full. Then He gave them a commandment to love one another, just as He had loved them.

6. Next, Jesus told them that they were no longer "servants," but He was now positioning them as "friends."

7. Next, He warned them that the world would hate them as it had hated Him. He was making it clear that they would represent Him on the earth and would have His power, but would also be persecuted as He was.

8. Jesus also stated several times throughout this discourse that whatever they asked of the Father in His name would be given to them. This was always written in the context of the fact that the Holy Spirit would be leading, guiding and teaching them. When we are led by the Spirit, we will ask what the Father wants us to ask and He will answer the prayers that He inspires us to pray.

9. In John 17, Jesus prays a wonderful prayer to His Father, in which He relates His purpose for coming to the earth and how much He desires His disciples to be successful after He is gone from them.

10. Finally, Jesus prays five specific prayers for unity among His disciples, who would quickly become His apostles, or

"sent ones." His passion for unity is really underestimated, but is the dominant theme in His prayer. Again, please allow me to highly recommend my book, *God's Favorite Number*. It's theme is unity and it reveals the power and the source of unity, based on John 17.

As we look at these teachings in the light of Communion, I believe we can see that The Lord's Table was a clear visual aid to help remember what He had just told them.

He was clearly revealing to them in a very profound way that He loved them so much that He was sharing everything with them and partnering with them so that they could have a very real share in all the joys and rewards that He would receive from His Father in Heaven.

That started with His preparing mansions for them close to His. Then He gave them the vine and branches analogy, where the branches depend on the vine to bring life to them from the ground up. Everything He shared is talking about interdependency, love, joy, peace and unity, along with His provision of comfort, power, anointing and access to the Father, Himself, through His name, which they were authorized to use.

Finally, as He shared the bread and wine with them, dividing up one loaf and drinking from one cup, He made it a little more vivid and visual. His body would be sacrificed that night, but before it was, Jesus was giving it to them in the bread. His blood would be shed that night, but before it was, He was giving it to them in the wine.

It was like Jesus was saying to them, "They plan to kill my body and spill my blood on the ground, but before they can do that, I am giving both my gifts and my anointing to you to empower you to be My body with the Holy Spirit life of my blood flowing through your veins."

My heart is stirred as I actually see this for the very first time. All I can say, is, "WOW GOD!!! You are always a big step ahead of the enemy!!! Just when he thinks he's got You, You have already outfoxed him and turned his apparent victory into a stunning and fabulous defeat.

THE PROPHETIC ASPECT OF COMMUNION

"Then He said to them, 'With fervent desire I have desired to eat this Passover with you before I suffer; for I say to you, I will no longer eat of it until it is fulfilled in the kingdom of God.'

Then He took the cup; and gave thanks, and said, 'Take this cup and divide it among yourselves, for I say to you, I will not drink of the fruit of the vine until the kingdom of God comes.'" (Luke 22:15-18)

As we can see from the above passage, Jesus is well aware that great suffering awaits Him. However, even though He is not looking forward to the suffering, He has passionately desired to celebrate this Passover with His disciples.

This passionate desire, I believe, is because it would be the last opportunity for Jesus to share the deeper thoughts and burdens of His heart for them. It would give Him the forum to prepare them for what was coming; the painful as well as the exciting. It would also be the time for Him to prophetically transfer His ministries and Holy Spirit anointing to them.

But, if I may use my imagination a little, I wouldn't be a bit surprised if He was already thinking about the future Kingdom, where He would rule and reign together with His disciples on the earth for a thousand years. Let's take a look together at what that might look like and how it would play out.

When Jesus eats the bread and drinks the wine in His Kingdom, we will be there with Him, enjoying again a celebration of the Passover. Conditions on the earth will be radically changed from the way they were then and the way they are now.

We know that the devil will be bound and cast into a bottomless pit for a thousand years. How does that relate to the Passover meal?

The Passover meal took place as the last meal in Egypt, where they had been kept in bondage. The Passover meal was a reminder of the fact that the Angel of Death had passed over their home and spared their firstborn children. In addition, it was a reminder that their sins would be covered by the blood sacrifice of the lamb they were to eat. It was also a celebration of victory over their enemies, who were not so fortunate.

Thus, a celebration in the Kingdom of Heaven on the earth, with Jesus ruling and reigning, and with us at His side, will be a celebration of God's power over our enemy and the fact that he has been defeated by the miraculous power of God. When we eat and drink together, we will be rejoicing that we have been freed from the bondage brought on by our slave master, the devil, and we will rejoice in the fact that Jesus blood broke the power of that bondage, and we as His body are now completed by the fact that the Head of the body has actually been fully reunited with His body on the earth.

Therefore, when we celebrate Communion now, we can not

only rejoice in the ministries and gifts He has given us, and the power of the Holy Spirit which flows through His body, but we can also look forward to the great reunion and restoration of the fullness of the body of Christ and the joy of being delivered from our enemy, who has been bound for one thousand years. What a celebration that will be!

SUMMARY

I really had no idea how rich the revelation on this subject would be when I started this chapter. But let's summarize what we've learned here:

Freed from the shadows of the Dark Ages, we can clearly see that Jesus was truly imparting an incredible and wonderful truth when He shared the bread and the wine with His disciples. He was telling them that His body and His blood was given "for them." He was imparting, with this analogy, His power to do signs and wonders, and all His gifts and ministries. He was also imparting all the anointing from the Holy Spirit, the very same Holy Spirit Who had filled Him at the River Jordan, before He began His ministry.

They would not only carry His message, the good news of the Kingdom, but they would also have the same power and do the same miracles and even more than He did, because He was sending them the same Source of power that worked through His physical body on the earth. When they ate the bread and drank the wine, they were to remember what He had just taught them in John 14-17. They now had a visual aid to remind them and it would give them strength, courage and joy as they celebrated what He had given them.

Remember, most of the feasts of the Old Covenant were times of celebration and they were literally feasts. As Nehemiah and the other leaders reminded the people during the days of restoration, the "holy day" was to be a time to "eat the fat and drink the sweet." It was a time to celebrate and send gifts to those who had needs.

And finally, we can see that celebrating the Passover Communion in the coming Kingdom of Heaven on the earth will be a time of celebrating a freedom, not only from the power and punishment of our sin, but even from the source of our temptation. What a joyous celebration that will be!

I trust that celebrating Communion will never be the same again for you. I know I can't go back to the somber and heavy ceremony that I was raised up with. It will always be for me a time of great joy and thankfulness and a time to commit to Jesus, that the gift of His body and His blood will not be in vain in my life and ministry. Instead, I want to be a good steward of the precious gifts that He has placed in my life.

Maybe you would like to pray this prayer with me:

Precious Jesus, my Savior and Lord,

How I love you and worship you for your incredible and generous sacrifice on my behalf! Truly, You have given me more than I have ever comprehended or ever deserved. I am overwhelmed by you goodness to me. Please help me to discern your body and appreciate the blood you shed for me. And please help me to be a faithful steward of every precious gift you have given me to use to build Your Kingdom. Please, Jesus, forgive me for any time that I have used Your gifts to make a name for myself or marketed it to build my own ministry or my own kingdom.

I commit my life and ministry, my gifts and callings to build

your Kingdom, and whatever territory You give to me to adminis-
trate for You, please help me to do it completely and totally for Your
glory and honor.

I pray this in Your wonderful and powerful name, Jesus, and
for Your glory,

Amen!

Chapter Seven

The Blessings of Baptism

Most Christians are aware of the various debates in Christianity over the practice of baptism. The key debates focus on methods, such as sprinkling or immersion, and in whose name they are to be baptized.

Like all the subjects discussed in this book, church leaders have often focused on aspects that mean much less to God than they do to the people who run religions. It's true that baptism means immersion and that Jesus spoke one thing and the apostles did another regarding the "in the name of" part of the baptism. Thus, it is legitimate to ask the question, "What is the correct way to do baptism.

However, as always, God isn't that worried about what religious formula we use, since God always looks at the heart, not the externals. Doing things right doesn't make us more holy or accepted by God.

Even going back to Cain and Abel, there is really no evidence that God was upset with Cain because he offered grain instead of an animal. It's true that the shedding of an animal's blood was later used as a symbol of the Lamb of God, Who would shed His blood for our sins. But God also called for offerings of grain and other produce of the field in the Law of Moses. My guess is that Cain had a bad attitude towards God, for some reason or another and did not offer his sacrifice with a pure heart. Of course, we have no evidence either way, but we can see how he responded to Abel and to the judgment that God spoke over him. He was really a self-centered man and had issues of pride, self-pity and anger.

Understanding Baptism

But let's get back to baptism. We know that Jesus came to John to be baptized in the Jordan. John protested, saying,

> *"I need to be baptized by You, and are You coming to me?"*
> *But Jesus answered and said to him, "Permit it to be so*
> *now, for thus it is fitting for us to fulfill all righteousness."*
> *Then he allowed him. (Matthew 3:14,15)*

Why did He do it? His explanation to John has been interpreted as, "I'm doing this just as an example so others will do it as well." But that's not really what He said. He said it was fitting or appropriate for us (which included Him) to do this to fulfill all righteousness. He didn't say, "this is a pattern for others to follow."

In what way, then, would Jesus be fulfilling all righteousness by being baptized? I believe that He was being an example to us, but in a different way than we have perceived. We need a little better understanding of the purpose and tradition of baptism to understand what was going on here.

If you're looking for a single word or two to describe the meaning of baptism, it would be, "Commitment" or "Promise." Baptism was a means by which a person would make a public proclamation that they were becoming a disciple of someone, because they wanted to learn from the Master or become known as one of His disciples, for their own personal benefit. It could also mean that they were making a commitment to a new way of life, as with John, the Baptist, when he offered a baptism of repentance. Those who were baptized were saying that they were committed to change their ways and be ready for the coming of the Messiah, Who would bring them the Kingdom of God.

Cost of Discipleship

We know a man who was a disciple of Frank Lloyd Wright, the famous Chicago skyline architect. I don't believe Mr. Wright baptized the man, but he did bring him and others into his home and taught them for a period of weeks or months. He and the others were in the house throughout the Christmas holiday season and none of them were allowed to leave and go home during that time. He required a serious commitment from them if they were to claim that they were taught and discipled by him.

Even so, discipleship with Jesus was described as a serious affair. Jesus made numerous statements about the requirements for discipleship. First of all, they had to forsake everything and follow Him. Secondly, they were told they would have to take up their own crosses and follow Him. They did pretty well on the first requirement, but they failed miserably when tested on the second. However, Jesus knew their hearts and immediately forgave them and spoke peace to them. Then immediately He promoted them and "apostled" them, saying, "As the Father has sent Me, I also send you." (John 20:21) The word, "apostle," means, "sent one."

Was Jesus a Disciple?

Okay, that's a little foundation. Let's build on that. If baptism was the commitment of a disciple to His master or to a new way of life, how did that apply to Jesus? Was Jesus going to submit Himself to a Master, when He, Himself, was the Master? The answer is YES!

Jesus did not come to earth as God, but as the Son of Man. He left behind many of His Royal privileges and rights. Instead, He humbled Himself and came to earth as a man and as a servant (See Philippians 2:5-11). So, if He was a servant, Who was His Master? Obviously, His Master was His Father in Heaven, Who had retained all His Royal Majesty. In addition, He came to be a servant to humanity and shed His blood for them.

Fulfilling All Righteousness

For Jesus, righteousness was simply pleasing and obeying His Father in Heaven. He made that so clear, especially all through-out the book of John. Jesus was going to fulfill the pattern of a disciple as a public proclamation that He was a follower of His Father and was willing to do everything His Father had asked Him to do.

Jesus knew the purpose of His mission on the earth. He

knew the cross, with all its physical, mental and emotional pain and suffering, was awaiting Him. Baptism was a symbol of death to an old way of living and then rising up to embrace a new way of living.

Jesus, in baptism, fulfilling the righteousness of pleasing and obeying His Father, was saying, "Yes, Father, I will die for these people, knowing that they don't deserve it. But I am making a public statement that I will lay my life down, putting Myself in human hands, knowing that You will raise me up again, and bring me into a new place of honor with you."

THE TRUE IMPORTANCE OF BAPTISM

Instead of thinking of baptism as a religious ritual that new Christians should go through to assure their salvation (as some do), we ought to really embrace the meaning of it in a personal way. For Jesus, it was reaffirming His commitment as a human being, which He had made in Heaven in the presence of His Father. That commitment was that He would die and be raised again into a new way of life, which for Him was a return to Heaven, where He would receive even more honor and glory, because of what He had done. (Isaiah 53:12, Philippians 2:9-11)

In the light of this example, I am convinced that we should impress on new Christians, who want to be baptized, that they are making a commitment to God, that they are willing to lay down their lives for Jesus, as He did for them. And I mean to literally live and die for Him if faced with the situation.

Before we get into the heart of this subject—the Blessings of Baptism—let's clear up one little issue, which has been debated by many religious leaders.

In the Name Of

One of the biggest, but least important debate is over the formula that we speak at baptism. The question is: "Should we do what Jesus told us to do in Matthew 28:19, and other passages, or should we do what the apostles did, who should have known what Jesus meant?

Jesus said to baptize in the name of the Father, Son and Holy Spirit. The apostles baptized in the name of Jesus. Is one right and the other wrong? Did Jesus make a mistake, or did the disciples mess up? Or did neither of them get it wrong?

Some argue that Jesus IS the name of the Father, Son and Holy Spirit, since Father and Holy Spirit are titles, rather than names. It is interesting however, that in Isaiah 9:6, we are told that HIS NAME shall be called Wonderful, Counselor, Mighty God, Everlasting Father, Prince of Peace. These are all titles, but Isaiah says they are His names.

However, this really isn't that complicated. To do something in someone else's name simply means you have their authority and you are representing them. Jesus told them that they had the authority of the full "Godhead." The apostles had been told by Jesus to baptize, so they were saying that they got their authority from Jesus. It's really all a big argument over nothing, and I believe it was inspired by a religious spirit to keep us fighting over insignificant things and prolong the divisions in the body of Christ.

The Glorious and Bountiful
Blessings of Baptism

Why did the Jews flock to the Jordan to be baptized by John? Why did so many people follow Jesus and desire to be His disciples? Why would they be willing to leave everything behind and travel around the country with Him? Why would a young, budding architect give up his time with his family during Christmas to be a disciple of Frank Lloyd Wright?

1. Excitement of a New Life Awaiting

Although, baptism represented death to the old ways of living for self, it also represented a new life free from the pain and penalties of the old life. It represented a forsaking of the old ways, but it also represented the new pathways that were so much more exciting than the old boring and disappointing pathways.

Baptism in the Jordan was a dip in cool refreshing and cleansing waters. It is an exhilarating experience to come out of a dip in cool waters. The moment of going under is soon forgotten as you feel the joy of the past being forgiven and forgotten and a new beginning awaiting you.

2. Privilege of Being Accepted or Chosen as a Disciple of a Great Master

Consider the thrill of being accepted as a student by the world's greatest pianist or flautist or trumpet player, if you had a passion to go to the top as a player of one of those instruments. Or think about the privilege of being chosen by the world's best swimming coach if you had Olympic Gold aspirations. You would know that he or she had the confidence that you could be the greatest, or they wouldn't waste their time on you.

Now think about the privilege of being taught and empowered by the most powerful Being in the universe to know many of His secrets and do the same things that He does, using extraordinary means to accomplish incredible things. That would be you and I, who are called to rule and reign with King Jesus on this earth for a thousand years and then live with Him forever in eternal bliss.

In addition, think of the awesome privilege of being able to "hang out" with the most powerful and all-knowing kings and leaders in the universe. We have been given instant and constant access to the throne room and the courts of the King's palace and we can listen in to the Royal conversations if we learn to listen with our spiritual ears.

How could we even think of calling it a "sacrifice" to give up a few earthly things to enjoy such amazing privileges and achieve such incredible eternal accomplishments and accumulate such unbelievable and unimaginable rewards? In a moment of thinking in the flesh, I could say, "You know, I've really sacrificed a lot to serve Jesus. I could have gone a long ways in business or engineering or anything else I put my mind to. I could have made a lot of money and had a great retirement income."

What rubbish! God has given me so much more than anyone with a big bank account who isn't serving Jesus. I've had the awesome privilege of seeing God do incredible miracles, sometimes using me and sometimes using others. I've seen deaf ears hear and blind eyes see. I've seen people healed of cancer, deformities and many other physical conditions. Recently I witnessed a gal healed of a torn meniscus and a torn ACL at the same time.

Another very exciting thing for me is the fact that through the supernatural power of God to touch people's hearts, giving them faith to believe, I've seen thousands either saved or restored to a living relationship with God. Many have said, "YES!" to the call of God on their lives to use their God-given gifts and talents for His glory. Today, as a father of five, a grandfather of eleven, and a spiritual father to many more, I have received so much honor from those we have served that I feel extremely fulfilled and gratified here on the earth.

For me, one of the most exciting rewards for being a disciple of Jesus, and hanging out with Him is to experience the anointing on my preaching and teaching, including when I'm writing a book like this. It is a thrill beyond words to know that the Holy Spirit is speaking His words through my mouth, or in this case, through my fingers on the keyboard. (See Isaiah 51:16, 59:21, Jeremiah 1:9, I Peter 4:11)

However, the most exciting rewards by far still await me in Heaven. Because of the privilege Brenda and I have had of praying for and speaking and prophesying to thousands, and because my books have taught many that I've never met, I anticipate being blessed by many more in Heaven.

Is it any wonder that I don't have any hesitation in suggesting that anyone take advantage of the offer of the Master to become His disciple? Who, in their right minds, would not jump at the chance? As Paul declared, any suffering in this life is in no way worthy to be compared with the rewards that we will receive in the next. But even now, I have such amazing fulfillment and joy, doing what I do for free. That means, I get blessed without paying for the blessings and I serve others without them paying for my service to them. It's called grace and it is an incredible free gift from God to share with others.

Chapter Eight

Application of Revelation

The number eight represents new beginnings as we mentioned earlier. This brief chapter will focus on taking new steps to apply what we have discovered in the first seven chapters.

1. Be on the Lookout for Dark Ages "Stinking Thinking"

We don't easily change the way we think when we've thought the same for a long, long time. Keep the light on and watch out for shadows of past darkness to encroach on your freedom and joy. Watch out for the religious spirit, for traditions of men and for heaviness and depression, brought on by a spirit of guilt and condemnation.

Remember, God loves you for who you are—His child, created in His image. He is not looking to judge you, even though He may give you a "direction correction" from time to time to keep you on the pathway of peace. He dearly wants to bless you as every normal parent wants to bless his or her child. Open your heart and accept His unconditional love.

2. Enjoy the Privilege of Being "Holy" to the Lord.

You are chosen to be special and unique and filled with the very nature of your God, through your intimate relationship with the Father, Son and Holy Spirit. Listen to His voice for direction and wisdom, rather than accepting the traditional wisdom of religious tradition.

3. Review the Suggestions Regarding the Sabbath and the First Day (which we covered in Chapter Five)

Don't get legalistic. I don't! Just see if God will give you some creative ideas to give your body and mind a break from the normal and then ask Him for ideas to give Him a tithe of your time in dedicated service to build His Kingdom.

4. Regarding Communion, remind yourself, as often as you do it, that His death and resurrection accomplished so much more for us than we have acknowledged in the past.

Thank Him for the gifts and ministries that He divided up in His body, and that He didn't leave you out. Commit to Him that you will be a good steward of these gifts and ministries. Also, remember the importance of the teaching about the body of Christ and the other things Jesus spoke about in John 14-17.

The key points to remember are listed in Chapter Six, but probably the most important is the fact that He wants us to be intimately dependent on Him and on one another. We need to be the "ONE BODY AND ONE BREAD" that Paul talked about in I Corinthians 10.

5. Finally, don't forget what we learned in the previous chapter on Baptism.

It's more than a ceremony or confirmation of our decision to become a Christian. It's accepting an invitation to become a disciple of the greatest Master that ever lived. It's a greater honor than becoming a student of Mozart or Michelangelo or Warren Buffet. Baptism is truly an open door into an amazing new life.

In conclusion, let me say how great a privilege and honor it is for me that you have read this book and allowed the Holy Spirit to touch you through it. It is such a blessing to me when people tell me their lives were changed by the truths they have read in our books. If you want to write me, you can email me at: *ohmint@gmail.com*. I will try to reply to all correspondence.

About Ben Peters

BEN R. PETERS has been a student of the Word since he could read it for himself. He has a heritage of grandparents and parents who lived by faith and taught him the value of faith. That faith has produced many miracle answers to prayer in their family life. Ben and Brenda have founded a ministry in northern Illinois called Kingdom Sending Center.

They also travel extensively world-wide, teaching and ministering prophetically to thousands annually. Their books are available on most ereaders and all other normal book outlets, as well as their website: *www.kingdomsendingcenter.org*

A Mandate to Laugh
Overcoming the Sennacherib Spirit
by Ben R. Peters

Available from Kingdom Sending Center
www.kingdomsendingcenter.org

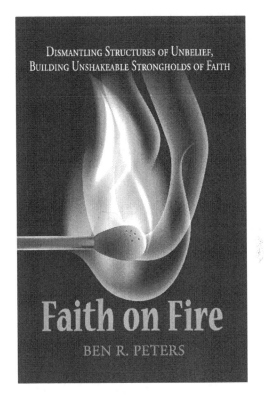

Faith on Fire
Dismantling Structures of Unbelief,
Building Unshakeable Strongholds of Faith
by Ben R. Peters

Available from Kingdom Sending Center
www.kingdomsendingcenter.org

Humility and How I *Almost* Achieved It
Uncovering a Highly Valued Key
to Lasting Success and Kingom Power
by Ben R. Peters

Available from Kingdom Sending Center
www.kingdomsendingcenter.org

The Boaz Blessing
Releasing the Power of This Ancient Blessing
Into Your World Today
by Ben R. Peters

Available from Kingdom Sending Center
www.kingdomsendingcenter.org

"The Ultimate Convergence is imminent and I am excited with all that God is going to do." ~ Dr. C. Peter Wagner

BEN R. PETERS

The Ultimate Convergence
An End Times Prophecy of the Greatest
Shock and Awe Display Ever to Hit Planet Earth
by Ben R. Peters

Available from Kingdom Sending Center
www.kingdomsendingcenter.org

**Veggie Village and the Great
and Dangerous Jungle**
An Allegory
by Ben R. Peters

Available from Kingdom Sending Center
www.kingdomsendingcenter.org

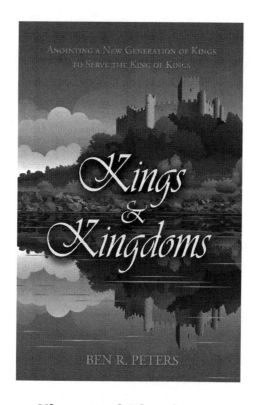

Kings and Kingdoms
Anointing a New Generation of Kings
to Serve the King of Kings
by Ben R. Peters

Available from Kingdom Sending Center
www.kingdomsendingcenter.org

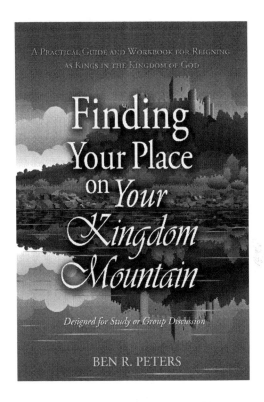

Finding Your Place
on Your Kingdom Mountain
A Practical Guide and Workbook for Reigning
as Kings in the Kingdom of God
by Ben R. Peters

Designed for Study or Group Discussion

Available from Kingdom Sending Center
www.kingdomsendingcenter.org

Catching up to the Third World
Seven Indispensable Keys
To EXPLOSIVE Revival
in the Western Church
by Ben R. Peters

Available from Kingdom Sending Center
www.kingdomsendingcenter.org

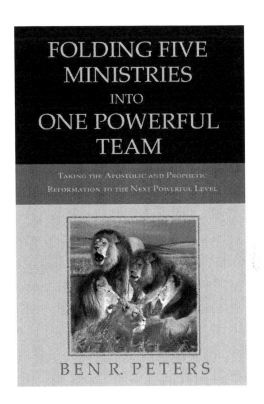

**Folding Five Ministries Into
One Powerful Team**
Taking the Apostolic and Prophetic Reformation
to the Next Powerful Level
by Ben R. Peters

Available from Kingdom Sending Center
www.kingdomsendingcenter.org

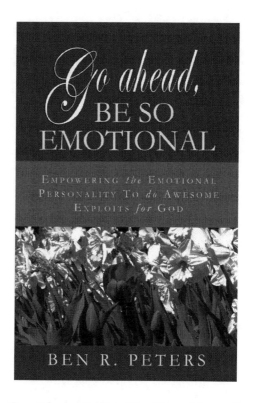

Go Ahead, Be So Emotional
Empowering the Emotional Personality
to do Awesome Exploits for God
by Ben R. Peters

Available from Kingdom Sending Center
www.kingdomsendingcenter.org

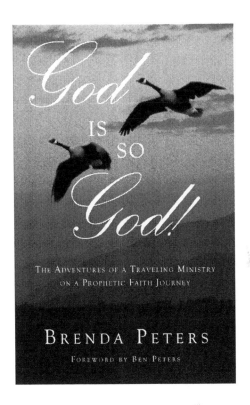

God Is So God!
The Adventures of a Traveling Ministry
on a Prophetic Faith Journey
by Brenda Peters

Available from Kingdom Sending Center
www.kingdomsendingcenter.org

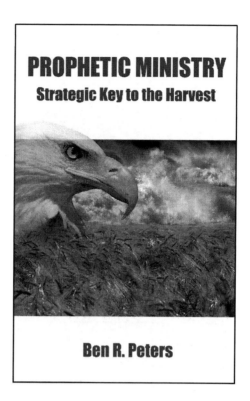

Prophetic Ministry
Strategic Key to the Harvest
by Ben R. Peters

Available from Kingdom Sending Center
www.kingdomsendingcenter.org

Resurrection!
A Manual for Raising the Dead
by Ben R. Peters

Available from Kingdom Sending Center
www.kingdomsendingcenter.org

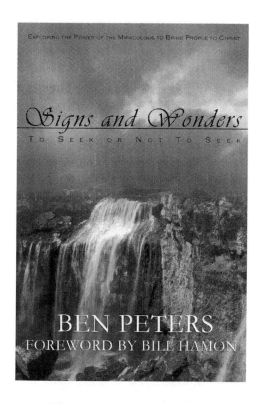

EXPLORING THE POWER OF THE MIRACULOUS TO BRING PEOPLE TO CHRIST

Signs and Wonders
TO SEEK OR NOT TO SEEK

BEN PETERS
FOREWORD BY BILL HAMON

Signs and Wonders
To Seek or Not to Seek
by Ben R. Peters

Available from Kingdom Sending Center
www.kingdomsendingcenter.org

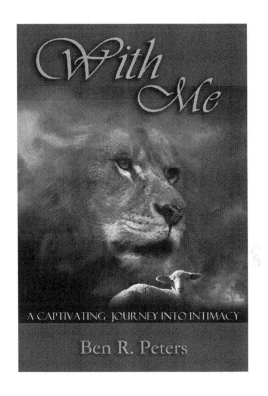

With Me
A Captivating Journey Into Intimacy
by Ben R. Peters

Available from Kingdom Sending Center
www.kingdomsendingcenter.org

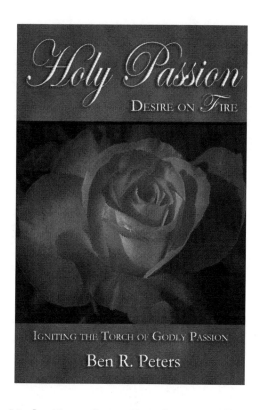

Holy Passion: Desire on Fire
Igniting the Torch of Godly Passion
by Ben R. Peters

Available from Kingdom Sending Center
www.kingdomsendingcenter.org

Birthing the Book Within You
Inspiration and Practical Help
to Produce Your Own Book
by Ben R. Peters

Available from Kingdom Sending Center
www.kingdomsendingcenter.org

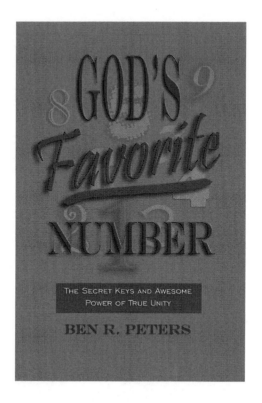

God's Favorite Number
The Secret Keys and Awesome
Power of True Unity
by Ben R. Peters

Available from Kingdom Sending Center
www.kingdomsendingcenter.org

Made in the USA
Charleston, SC
13 January 2016